CAROL McDOUGALL

Jellies in the Belly

A sea turtle's Atlantic adventure

BOULDER BOOKS

© 2022 Carol McDougall

Library and Archives Canada Cataloguing in Publication

Title: Jellies in the belly : a sea turtle's journey / Carol McDougall.
Names: McDougall, Carol, author.
Identifiers: Canadiana 2022024068X | ISBN 9781989417638 (hardcover)
Subjects: LCSH: Leatherback turtle—Juvenile literature. | LCSH: Leatherback turtle—Migration—Juvenile literature.
Classification: LCC QL666.C546 M33 2022 | DDC j597.92/89—dc23

Published by Boulder Books
Portugal Cove-St. Philip's, Newfoundland and Labrador
www.boulderbooks.ca

Design and layout: Tanya Montini
Editor: Stephanie Porter
Copy editor: Iona Bulgin

Printed in Canada

Excerpts from this publication may be reproduced under licence from Access Copyright, or with the express written permission of Boulder Books Ltd., or as permitted by law. All rights are otherwise reserved and no part of this publications may be reproduced, stored in a retrieval system, or transmitted in any form or by any means, electronic, mechanical, photocopying, scanning, recording, or otherwise, except as specifically authorized.

We acknowledge the financial support of the Government of Newfoundland and Labrador through the Department of Tourism, Culture, Arts and Recreation.

To everyone
who inspires wonder
and a love of nature.

Lally the leatherback hatchling looked up through the clutch of cracked eggs toward the moonlit sky. All of her sisters were coming up through the sand.

Inside the nest, nearly 100 female leatherback sea turtles worked together to get to the ocean.

Scooching around a plastic bottle and persisting through the break of a wave, the leatherback's trek had begun for ...

jellies in the belly. Swim far sea turtle, swim far.

5

Lally the small leatherback swam as she sampled her first taste of plankton. The warm salt water sloshed the leatherback, moving her away from her sisters as she struggled past the beaks of preying birds.

Lally was growing bigger and hungrier and was drawn to the deeper ocean with its promise of ...

jellies in the belly. Swim far sea turtle, swim far.

Colourful fish swam into the nets of tropical
fishers. Lally the growing leatherback watched
a male leatherback struggle to untangle himself.
Unable to swim backwards out of the net,
he allowed a fisher to help.

"Go eat more jellyfish and save our fish, lovely
leatherback." The fisher smiled, and added ...

jellies in the belly. Swim far sea turtle, swim far.

Lally the leatherback swam into the deep ocean.
She opened her toothless mouth wide and used
her spiny throat to catch larger and larger jellyfish.

Lured by the most interesting jellyfish she had ever
seen, Lally narrowly missed making a fatal mistake.
Instead of swallowing garbage, she chose …

jellies in the belly. Swim far sea turtle, swim far.

Swimming in tropical waters surrounded by helpful fish, Lally the leatherback spent almost five years searching the warm ocean for more ...

jellies in the belly. Swim far sea turtle, swim far.

Almost fully grown, Lally the leatherback swam north in a long journey to find bigger jellyfish. At last she saw signs of humans fishing in the colder water. Fish in the ocean meant ...

jellies in the belly. Swim far sea turtle, swim far.

One evening while she was sleeping on the surface of the ocean, Lally the leatherback did not notice a starving polar bear slip off an ice floe into the water. Suddenly, she felt its claws on her head.

The hunting polar bear did not notice the speeding boat which knocked the two of them apart.

The stunned polar bear climbed back on his ice floe, while the dizzy leatherback dove deep and continued her own hunt for more of those delicious ...

jellies in the belly. Swim far sea turtle, swim far.

A huge storm was brewing in the ocean.
Tired and wounded, Lally the leatherback
rested and felt the webbed feet of a puffin
on her back. Puffins eat fish, which are
more abundant when leatherbacks eat …

jellies in the belly. Swim far sea turtle, swim far.

Suddenly, a giant wave slammed the sea turtle onto the rocky shore. Weakened and stranded, Lally the leatherback looked up into the caring eyes of a Maritime man and his daughter.

After they called for help, people arrived to tend to her wounds. One person phoned scientists on a boat to watch out for her. They all helped her return to the sea to find more ...

jellies in the belly. Swim far sea turtle, swim far.

The next day, a research boat arrived to observe Lally the leatherback. The scientists examined her and tagged her to track her travels in the ocean by satellite.

They watched the leatherback swim toward her nesting beach. It was time to head south for those tropical ...

jellies in the belly. Swim far sea turtle, swim far.

Lally the leatherback had been alone for a very long time but continued to fill her belly with jellies, keeping the ocean habitat healthy.

As she searched for a mate, perhaps Lally used the sun, moon, and stars to guide her home, or maybe the pink spot on her head worked like a skylight or a compass. Somehow, she knew where to go to dive deep for more ...

jellies in the belly. Swim far sea turtle, swim far.

25

Finally, Lally the leatherback looked up and saw
a male swimming above her. After their mating,
she swam alone toward her tropical beach.

Along with hundreds of other female leatherbacks,
she rode the bubbly surf to shore to lay her eggs,
with the hope that they would always have ...

                                              jellies in the belly. Swim far sea turtle, swim far.

Lally the leatherback weighed half a tonne. She struggled to drag herself out of the ocean onto the clean sandy beach to dig her nesting hole and lay her clutch. After she flicked the last mound of sand over her eggs with her back flippers, it was time to find more jellyfish to eat.

With two slow blinks she released extra salt from her body in giant tears and scooched slowly across the moonlit beach toward the soothing ocean.

In about two months, her hatchlings would dig their way out and begin their own journey for ...

jellies in the belly. Swim far sea turtle, swim far.

The hatchling looked up through the clutch of eggs and all his brothers toward the moonlit sky. Like all male leatherbacks, he would never return to land.

Starting anew, under the watchful eyes of helpful humans, he scrabbled upward toward the sea for ...

jellies in the belly. Swim far sea turtle, swim far.

Did You Know?

Page 4   Sand temperatures determine if sea turtle eggs become male or female. Rising temperatures may increase the birth rates of female leatherbacks. To help conserve this endangered species, humans will need to help lower world temperatures so that more males can be born.

Page 6   Although plankton may be one of the first foods leatherbacks eat, jellyfish are their favourite food. Too many jellyfish is a sign of an unhealthy habitat, and jellyfish overeat young fish. Protecting leatherbacks helps to protect fish too.

Page 8   About 60 per cent of leatherbacks that feed near Newfoundland come from Trinidad nesting grounds.

Bernard Dupont, CC BY-SA 2.0

Page 10   Reducing the amount of plastics that pollute our oceans saves leatherbacks.

Page 12   Remora fish have a sucker to attach themselves to a larger host animal such as a leatherback. While they receive leatherback protection, these fish remove parasites and flakes of skin from the leatherback.

Page 14   Leatherbacks have the widest range of all sea turtles and are found swimming in oceans around the world (see map on pages 38–39). Scientists estimate that leatherbacks live from 30 to 100 years, but their age is still unknown.

Page 16   Huge adult leatherbacks have few predators but are sometimes preyed on by whales or sharks. Hungry polar bears on ice floes have started to hunt animals not normally considered their prey and could attack leatherbacks.

Page 18   The leatherback shell, with its seven ridges, is semi-flexible and covered in tough, oily tissue; this means that both bird and leatherback sense each other. Being unable to pull their head into their shell means that they cannot swim backwards or protect themselves like other land turtles.

Page 20   The non-profit group Whales Release & Strandings (newfoundlandlabradorwhales.net) helps distressed marine animals in Newfoundland and Labrador.

Alastair Rae, CC BY-SA 2.0

Page 22 Canadian Sea Turtle Network (seaturtle.ca) is a charity based in Nova Scotia which tracks and conserves sea turtles in Canada and beyond.

Page 24 Scientists are not sure how leatherbacks navigate to their nesting grounds but they believe that the distinctive pink spot on their heads acts like a skylight to keep in rhythm with seasons.

Page 26 Males may never return to land after leaving the beach as hatchlings.

Page 28 Leatherbacks release excess salt from their bodies in what looks like tears.

Page 30 You can make positive changes to help leatherbacks by removing plastics from beaches and helping people learn more about leatherbacks.

Elise Peterson, CC BY 3.0

Can you find?

A number of jellyfish species are seen in this book. Look back at the paintings. Can you find:

- Southern moon jellyfish
- Spot-winged comb jellyfish
- Moon jellyfish
- Four-handed box jellyfish
- Lion's mane jellyfish
- White cross jellyfish
- Mauve stinger
- Portuguese man o'war

Southern moon jellyfish

Four-handed box jellyfish

White cross jellyfish

Mauve stinger

Spot-winged comb jellyfish

Portuguese man o'war

Lion's mane jellyfish

Moon jellyfish

Create Jellies in the Belly Leatherback Art

Gather your art supplies. You will need:

- pencil and eraser
- watercolour paints
- salt
- permanent markers (including black, brown, pink, and metallic silver)
- watercolour paper
- paintbrush
- container to hold water

Work on a surface that you can get a bit wet.

Using the pencil, lightly draw the shield-shaped leatherback sea turtle shell. Add front and back flippers. Add the triangular-shaped head.

Use a pink marker to add the pink spot and a brown marker for the eyes. Use a black marker to colour in the rest of the leatherback.

Use the metallic silver marker to line the shell with five curved ridges (two of the seven ridges are hidden under the leatherback's sides). Add spots all over the shell, head, and flippers.

Add to your artwork. Draw yourself or ocean creatures in pencil and colour the images with permanent marker

Now it's time to use your paintbrush. Dip your brush into clean water and use it to wet the remaining paper, avoiding your drawings.

Choose colours to represent the sky and/or the ocean. Start painting strokes onto your wet paper to fill in the background.

While the paint is still wet, create a splashy water effect by lightly sprinkling salt over the painting. This only works with watercolour paint and paper. Allow your art to dry completely, then brush off the salt.

Finally, use the metallic silver marker to add in a jellyfish for your leatherback to eat and sign your artwork at the bottom corner.

Share your finished picture!

About the Author

CAROL MCDOUGALL, BEd, MA, is the Science in Society award-winning author/illustrator of *A Salmon's Sky View*. Carol, originally from Victoria, British Columbia, is an international educator, writer, and nature enthusiast living in St. John's, Newfoundland and Labrador.